To Give Life a Shape

Also from Gunpowder Press:
The Tarnation of Faust: Poems by David Case
Mouth & Fruit: Poems by Chryss Yost
Shaping Water: Poems by Barry Spacks
Original Face: Poems by Jim Peterson
Instead of Sadness: Poems by Catherine Abbey Hodges
What Breathes Us: Santa Barbara Poets Laureate, 2005-2015
Edited by David Starkey
Burning Down Disneyland: Poems by Kurt Olsson
Unfinished City: Poems by Nan Cohen
Raft of Days: Poems by Catherine Abbey Hodges

Shoreline Voices Projects:
Buzz: Poets Respond to SWARM
Edited by Nancy Gifford and Chryss Yost
Rare Feathers: Poems on Birds & Art
Edited by Nancy Gifford, Chryss Yost, and George Yatchisin

To Give Life a Shape

Poems Inspired by
the Santa Barbara Museum of Art

Edited by
David Starkey & Chryss Yost

Gunpowder Press • Santa Barbara
2017

© 2017 David Starkey & Chryss Yost

Cover Image: William Dole, *Tower of Babel*, 1962. Watercolor and collage on board. SBMA, Gift of Dean Valentine and Amy Adelson, Los Angeles

Published by Gunpowder Press
David Starkey, Editor
PO Box 60035
Santa Barbara, CA 93160-0035

ISBN-13: 978-0-9986458-2-7

www.gunpowderpress.com

Santa Barbara Museum of Art resources for teachers:
www.sbma.net/learn/lessonplans

About The Shoreline Voices Project: The Shoreline Voices Project publishes Santa Barbara-area poets writing on a specific theme. We thank the Santa Barbara Museum of Art, the curators, the artists, and Patsy Hicks for inspiring the poems in this collection.

Celebrating the
Santa Barbara Museum of Art

Contents

Steve Braff "Rakshasa" — 13
Delia Moon "Gwanyin at the Museum" — 14
RBS "Seated Luohan, China, Song-Yuan Dynasty, 13th Century" — 15
Pamela Davis "Wedding Vase: Cranes over Islands of Peach Trees, Early Qing Dynasty" — 17
John Ridland "The Secretary's Table" — 19
Glenna Luschei "Ride Down Santa Cruz Mountain" — 21
Peg Quinn "Boy On a Dock" — 22
Christina M. Pagés "Yearning" — 23
Mary Brown "Triolet for Carp Ascending a Waterfall" — 24
Enid Osborn "No Damage" — 25
Paul J. Willis "Art Is a Fire" — 27
Fran Davis "The Riverbank" — 29
Chryss Yost "All the New Enchantments" — 30
Alison M. Bailey "Her Name Was Lucy" — 31
Mary Freericks "Waterloo Bridge" — 32
John Chilcott "Waterloo Bridge" — 33
Rick Benjamin "The By-Product Storage Tanks" — 34
Emma Trelles "Winter Memoir" — 36
Daniel Thomas "The Old Bridge" — 37
Melinda Palacio "Mother's Golden Voice" — 38
Laure-Anne Bosselaar "From Her Favorite Bench in Ménérbes, Provence, Dora Maar, Aged 87, Feeds & Talks to the Pigeons at Her Feet" — 40
Linda Saccoccio "Beach Riders" — 42
John Elliott "Acts of Dis-conformity" — 43
Kathee Miller "While Looking at Chagall's Painting *Femme Cheval* at SBMA" — 44
Tessa Flanagan "The Casting of the Spell" — 47
Christine Penko "Dear Phyllis" — 49
Susan Shields "Questions for the Artist" — 50
Gabriella Josephine Klein "Mono Lake" — 51
Sojourner Kincaid Rolle "Simple Colors" — 52

Luci Janssen "Fragments"	54
Roslyn Strohl "Heritage"	56
Gudrun Bortman "Galaxy Apple"	57
Ronald A. Alexander "Black Panther Ghazal"	58
Perie Longo "Found You"	60
Kimbrough Ernest "Waves"	62
Patti Sullivan "Movement"	63
David Starkey "Bicentennial Bandwagon"	64
George Yatchisin "More Now to Be Innocent Of"	65
Kevin Patrick Sullivan "Monument for K.W."	67
Carol DeCanio "Brute"	68
Natalie D-Napoleon "Cementerio (Cemetery)"	70
Susan Chiavelli "Listen to the Ancestors"	72
Index of Artists & Poets	74

To Mean and To Be

A POEM SHOULD NOT MEAN
BUT BE.
—ARCHIBALD MACLEISH

Word and Image necessarily exist in an ongoing dance. But what happens when one art form is "translated" into another, when the visual inspires the verbal?

The formal name for this kind of writing is ekphrasis. The dictionary defines an ekphrastic poem as "a vivid description of a scene or, more commonly, a work of art. Through the imaginative act of narrating and reflecting on the 'action' of a painting or sculpture, the poet may amplify and expand its meaning."

For more than twenty years the Santa Barbara Museum of Art has invited local poets to do just that: to respond, redefine, rearrange, reflect and reveal the essence and experience of a visual work of art in language.

To Give Life a Shape is a collection of responses by local poets to work in the permanent collection of the SBMA. The anthology is coordinated, orchestrated and edited by former Santa Barbara Poets Laureate David Starkey and Chryss Yost and printed by their Santa Barbara-based publishing house, Gunpowder Press.

We hope this book will further inspire students, teachers, writers and artists to create, as the poet Edward Hirsch has suggested, their own "Imaginative acts of attention"; to look closely and even more closely at art and the world, and out of that observation create something new, a new form for remembering, representing, renaming experience; to revel in the interplay between image and word; in short, to mean and to be.

Patsy Hicks
Director of Education
Santa Barbara Museum of Art

Introduction

Commenting on a painting by Jean-Michel Basquiat, poet Adrian Matejka remarked that there is "something about the way visual imagery imprints—I can see the full version of the image or painting when I recall [it], not an emotional paraphrase or assessment. That immediacy lends itself to substantial conversations across the arts for me."

For those of us who are drawn to ekphrastic poetry—the rendering of a visual work in words—Matejka's contention that the "immediacy" of encountering a powerful painting (or photograph, or piece of sculpture) can result in a satisfying poem couldn't be more true.

Indeed, participating in readings inspired by images at the Santa Barbara Museum of Art has been an important part of the poetic lives of the editors of this book. Working over the past twenty years with Patsy Hicks, SBMA's long-time Director of Education, the two of us, as well as many dozens of our fellow local poets, have written about a range of works—both in temporary exhibitions and in the museum's permanent collection.

These readings have often resulted in brief pamphlets highlighting the poems and the paintings, but the three of us have long wanted to create a more permanent record of the "substantial conversations across the arts" that take place at the museum, and *To Give Life a Shape: Poems Inspired the Santa Barbara Museum of Art* is the result. The poems respond to works in the museum's permanent collection and have been written specifically for this anthology.

As past Poets Laureate of Santa Barbara, we have worked with Patsy to organize readings at the museum that have included many of the contributors to this book. The poets are from California's Central Coast, from Ventura to San Luis Obispo, but most live in Santa Barbara or neighboring Montecito and Goleta. They are, in short, the very people who visit the museum year-round, whether or not they are writing poems about its collections.

We believe the quote we have borrowed for our title from Jean Anouilh's play *The Rehearsal*—"The object of art is to give life a shape"—speaks to the way the poets have approached the works of art that inspired them. Whether they have envisioned themselves in the world of the paintings, or the images have evoked personal memories, the poets have given shape to both imagined and real life.

Ultimately, we hope those who read *To Give Life a Shape* will not only enjoy the poems in the book, but will also be inspired to join the long line of poets who have found so much pleasure in celebrating the visual arts.

> David Starkey and Chryss Yost
> Editors
> Gunpowder Press

Rakshasa

Eye
Garuda
Lord of Birds
volcano born
of morphed
hot molten
where
Java's lava
gone igneous hard
grey andesite stock
bound Man and Bird
a demon holy joined
this Guardian King
his headdress arch
stone stare eyes
all who walk
saw all that fly
so serpents did flee
his nose strong beak
though arms long gone
torso thick round ready
winged back held steady
mala wrap beads belt
on half lotus legged
toes turned talons
curl flex poised
in mudra rests
this museum
piece
Fly by—The years
Long past—Dare awaken
Lord Vishnu breathes—Life's power his prayer
Hindu God of Protection—Buddha Preserver of Good
Till Garuda's wings spread—Rock's crystal feather light
Hail Lord of Birds—Rakshasa takes flight

After *Garuda, the Man-Bird as a Guardian King*, Artist unknown (9c.-10c.)

Gwanyin at the Museum

Gwanyin, Bodhisattva
of Compassion turns
away, invites me to change
position to see her face, full face.
She stands upon a lotus
pad of purity, extends
in blessing her right hand upward
She seems to speak, to move
to me, her mouth full-lipped,
serene. She says stay. She says
I hear you and
I love you.

Her eyebrows arch over
almond, inward-seeing lids.
Her one dark eye, a marble, luminescent,
a pinpoint of soul-piercing light
to light us from the darkness of our pain.
I still see, she says, out of the marble I have lost.
With insight. There is no final loss.
Her quiet face, a face that knows
the suffering of all the unquiet world.
She absorbs it clear-eyed and calm,
radiating to all who stand before her—
as I do now, in homage and devotion—
deep peacefulness from a
place of utter stillness,
her deep, compassionate love.
Go, she says. Be me.

After *Standing Bodhisattva Guanyin, China, Jin Dynasty*, Unknown (1115-1234)

Seated Luohan, China, Song-Yuan Dynasty, 13th Century

O Lohan
do you still have your ferocious will
to penetrate to the essence,
through the single ego of so-called self
and its skandha heaps of name & form,
deluded by the false outfit
of all that we perceive
with naked senses still dusty?

Can you relax that furrowed brow
bound into tightness
unable to cut through the last fixation,
the emptiness of appearances,
the fear of no other?
What is your doubt about our true nature?
Will you seize the two-bladed sword
forged and tempered in the Akanishtha pure land
& slice through the imaginary obstacles
we hold so dear and substantial?

We are counting on you
the latest heart son of the lion of the Sakyas
as you take this final resolve
to wake again & again
through the watches of the night,
holding through the assaults
of the son of the gods, the endless accumulation of so many things,
the "evil one" of conflicting emotions, and
the temptation of neurotic destruction—
all raging and arrayed in horror & wielding the seductions and
ornaments

of lust and aggression.
Will you work with the negativity and
welcome the world of the nonspiritual?

Be strong.
Do not move.
Lead us beyond all the exhaustible and inexhaustible dharmas
past peace and confusion
through all the dualities…
Take us to the samadhi of majesty & play

Armed by the Mother of the Buddhas
with the Prajnaparamita,
hold firm, as a torch illuminating
the universe and all that is sunya.
Ride gently the breath into space
and carry us with you.
We are all only so many broken hearts
with no sense of direction
attempting to see through our salty tears.
But lo, if you hasten slowly
footprints are enough to guide us
on this path made golden by kindness…

Tenderly, with a gentle breeze
at our back
we will follow
as you arise without origin,
a gentler warrior to kiss the new morning,
the dawn of the Great Eastern Sun.

After *Seated Luohan, China, Song-Yuan dynasty, 13th century*, Unknown (13c.)

Wedding Vase: Cranes over Islands of Peach Trees, Early Qing Dynasty

The prosperous groom carefully unwinds the gift, round
    and round, bamboo wrap drifting to floor in ivory sheaves,
        his bride a whisper beside him. With the tips of her fingers

she traces the slender neck of the vase descending to rounded shoulders,
    wedged base, its porcelain womb. Round and round, cranes fly north
        to south, east to west, heaven to earth, a cerulean world of sea

and sky. The Immortal islands shimmer and blush, blossoms mutable as clouds
    that collapse to return as moon lanterns. Each crane dangles a gift
        tied with ribbons in its beak. The enamels dance as lightly

as the silk threads on her nuptial robes. A crane's mighty wingrush of air—
    she feels this—lofting to bear two burnished peaches across time. Round
        and round they soar proffering oranges, gold scrolls,

    baskets of fruit. Messengers of ancestral blessings—prosperity,
longevity, fecundity. Swept up,
the girl flushes, high color surfacing powdered cheek. A mortal bride bound

    for the wedding chamber, her head swims
    with promises made. The islands beckon. As she circles it,
the vase looms, clarifies like the Autumn moon. Round and round the
    cranes fly,

       wings flared, legs suspended in time, silent
as the breath artists take between paint and brush.

The birds' necks stretch beyond the hazes of heaven, generation unto
       generation.

She bites her nail. Unworldly girl, what must she yield to earn
       such good fortune?

After *Vase with Flying Cranes over Islands of Peach Trees*, Unknown (1735-1795)

The Secretary's Table

became through William Michael Harnett a *trompe l'oeil*
Still Life, and for the Preston Morton Collection
a prime acquisition in the year before I arrived
in Santa Barbara and checked out the Art Museum.
I never paid any attention to its bright
red stick of sealing wax propped up in the middle,
and all the rest, at rest on a marble slab—
a "Table"? A very very narrow table:
a red inkpot with a genuine feather quill
lightening the dark side of the scene;
a blue envelope, face down, sealed in red from the stick;
pencil and notepad, four names we can't read,
on a sloping stand of rich red wood, by a box
hinged from the end, its lid at an acute angle,
five fresh envelopes fanning out, a circular
"icon" (we'd call it) in their return-address corners.
A white, not ivory paper knife for envelopes,
and a candlestick, of satin finish brass,
a white candle burned down to an inch
and a whisk of black wick, and three inexplicable
red dots undeceiving our eyes: this is a flat canvas.
That's it. So what it wants of us is to make
us make some greater sense of it, as we sit
at our wide Mexican softwood dining table,
writing with a Paper Mate Ink Joy gel,
in a Moleskin Notebook—costly at Office Max,
cheap at Costco, where I bought a six-pack
for just this purpose: writing a *trompe l'oeil*,
or *trompe l'oreille*, since it's words deceive the ear.

Painting is for the eye, yet The Secretary's Table
cries out to be read in words, all the hidden words
that were written on it—in that envelope, face down,
which hides the addressee, being sealed in red.
(The sender's seal ring probably on his finger.)

I remember "The Secretary's Table" not from first sight
but because it was delivered to me on a postcard
from a friend under a "death threat" from melanoma—
so he told me in the Men's Room, abrupt as ever
like this painting now a message from the distant past.

After *The Secretary's Table,* William Michael Harnett (1870)

Ride Down Santa Cruz Mountain

Morning ride down
Santa Cruz Mountain.
On black earth
bright flowers grew:
lupin and poppy.

The road scared
me but Tom
my brother slammed
on brakes anyway
when he saw
the Century Plant
flowering great big
from the side.

We might slide
and wreck but
worth the danger
to see what
I can be
at one hundred.

After *Loma Prieta, Morning in the Santa Cruz Mountains,* William Keith
    (1874)

Boy On a Dock

He screams
delighted
imagining
stick and stone to
knife and bone
Leaps and yells
as warrior,
cowboy, soldier,
shouting orders
rolls through bedclothes,
beach, or grass while
exiting his launched
spacecraft
Bellows
with mouth full
as dinner roll
transforms
to dinosaur

Later, he stares off, sober dreamer,
sifting through mysteries, wondering
beyond light bouncing off water

After *Boy Fishing*, John George Brown (1877)

Yearning

I am Rosa Petronoff from St. Petersburg
immersed in Parisian romance,
but already tired of these men
with their grunts and gestures,
their knowledgeable nods
and mumbles from beards and whiskers
about marble breasts and thighs:
Indeed, my dear Sir, this sculpture
reveals the true essence of feminine beauty.

Rudolphus, my husband of five years,
barely looks at my body. At night,
under sheets, my curves remain his mystery.
By day, I must move my costumed form
across polished floors, through tapestried rooms
with the hope of raising an admiring
eyebrow or two.
Our reputation, my husband's approval,
depend on the grace of my covering.

I see a bend of the River Seine
through that window—
I will slip out tonight,
remove these layers,
uncover my young white body
for the moon.

After *Foreign Visitors to the Louvre,* James Tissot (1879-81)

Triolet for Carp Ascending a Waterfall

carp
thrusts
darts
carp
carves
up
carp
thrusts

zips
down
slips
unzips
silk
unbound
zips
down

After a Japanese stencil, Unknown (Late 19th-early 20th c.)

No Damage

Armless, headless,
half his chest ravaged,
and what of his heart?

He does not think to salvage
the rest. What part
would he retrieve?

For thus conceived, thus cast
was Art: Blind and blasted
under heaven!

But whole in the mind of Rodin.
And whole in the mind
of The Walking Man.

No damage here, no tears.
A soul is damned to walk
one hundred thirty-seven years

upon a single rock, forging
one path on legs of wrath.
Still, the armless muse

has no fear, does not stall
the merest moment to surmise
what he would stand to lose
if he should fall.

Other armless statues
began with arms and hands,
the headless had their eyes.

What sadness! Shattered in bombings
and quakes, harmed by some mistake
or fate or hammers of madness,

tossed in the elections. Dented,
lost, the perfections they were
meant to emulate.

All toppled from places high,
parted from their sex, their faces,
shorn of their graces in the fall.

Later, lovingly replaced upon the stand,
to mourn for an eternity the pretty hand,
the head, the breast, the frill.

Bereft of symmetry,
they hold whatever's left
perfectly still.

After *The Walking Man*, Auguste Rodin (1880)

Art Is a Fire

Art is a fire, for it burns the heart;
it is a phoenix from the ashes rising.
So do not think it can be felt in part,
a cheerful blaze upon the hearth, apprising
the viewer of some sweet domestic charm.

It is a conflagration on a slope
that sweeps like silent tidal waves, whose harm
we face without a single, embered hope
that we will ever be one whit the same.

Kinkade, you are a liar. We will go
where darkness visible makes Milton's flame,
where David's heat makes Michelangelo
to know the shape of shoulder in the stone.

Art is a pillar of the finest fire;
it leads us into exile, all alone,
where we must sacrifice upon the pyre
our smoldering flesh, the scorched and sooted bone.

Or if it lead us to a desert home,
it leads us where we do not wish to stray,
where broken statues lie inside the poem
and lone and level sands stretch far away.

Art is a fire, for it burns the heart;
it is a phoenix from the ashes rising.
So do not say it purifies in part;

we are consumed without our realizing
art is a fire, for it burns the heart.

After *Veracruz*, Thomas Moran (1885)

The Riverbank

Steadily she treads, lonely
along the riverbank, gaze fixed on
another woman far ahead, a black dog
like the one of her childhood--
memory of warmth and gleeful love.

The wind is in her face, bearing
a longed-for scent, tilting
the brim of her hat. She trails the dog,
clasping her hands and letting go,
clasping and letting go. Her hands work

in small waves with the river, carrying
her forward. The dog will lead her
to the sea where she will stop on the strand,
her eyes filled with enormity, vast and blue,
smothering all sorrows.

After *Herblay—The Riverbank,* Opus 24, Paul Signac (1889)

All the New Enchantments

"500 new fairytales were just discovered in Germany..." NPR

Things get better. Things get worse.
        Rescue happens just in time.
                New robes cloak the ancient curse.

The older the evil, the richer the rhyme—
        be careful the forces you summon in song.
                Everything listens here, more than it seems.

Many paths homeward, so many wrong.
        Clouds of crows gather—the murders disperse.
Many paths homeward, so many wrong.

                Everything watches here, more than it seems—
        an apple or rose where it doesn't belong—
the older the evil, the richer the broth.

                Be careful the forces you summon in song,
        old words wrapped in new found cloth.
Things get darker. Things get lost.

After *Castle in Moonlight*, Henri Rousseau (1889)

Her Name Was Lucy

Years of thunder-wind-sun-cloudless skies rainsculpt
 her ribs, her skull into abstract art
 for no one.

She—sweet, surefooted bay—finds heaven
 a bit dull. All those green hills, white high rivers
 tumble spray the bee-danced clover.

Praying, kneeling difficult for a horse. Ghost
 that she is her smoky bones remember all those sinking
 sand crossings,

those dry stream pebbles embedded in soft hooves. Wandering
 alongside Darwin they swap stories. He admits he was wrong.
 She allows him to ride her, bareback, free from the iron

bit on her tongue, lost. Both mumble disappointment
 in the unfortunate untruth of reincarnation.
 When she rests

she sees her cowboy weep as he undoes
 the cinch of her sweat-soaked saddle.
 Lucy died with her eyes open.

After *Fight over a Waterhole*, Frederick Remington (1897)

Waterloo Bridge

Waving over the blue-
turquoise water
is it a green sail?

Pink flowers
or sunset
in the sky
spreads across the water.

Now from the opposite end
of the gallery
I see the bridge.
I was too close before.

And a man
stands on the boat
that was just a green sail
before.

And I see sun streaming
through all the arches
of Waterloo Bridge.

After *Waterloo Bridge*, Claude Monet (1900)

Waterloo Bridge

your hand having checked the clasp, she drifts off toward the white wine, bare shoulders capping the rustle of her dress, and the part of you that stood farther inside now stands by a bridge on a winter day watching the water as the dusk daubs the crests with red scumbles of sun and fills the troughs with indigo, and from the dim outlines of smokestacks on the far bank a pale glow of fog arrives over the river, where the mists meet the breeze and mingle with the flattering patter of partygoers floating out from shore, pebbles and syllables rolling and retreating down the brown sand, the slack and slapping mossy wet ropes trailing over the swells to deck cleats and shoe heels echoing across the hardwood; a pleasing dislocation: you don't move as people walk by but smell the stuffed mushrooms steaming past under the bridge, dirtsmoke on the water, spiderwebs of lamplight stitching across the arches, the missing black unshackled into cobalt, leafy green, pewter and rose that grows across the sky, cigarette embers bobbing on the velvet backwaters of the river and the room, pillars coated with piano notes, cocktail glasses clinking against the sides of boats slowly rocking, voices swirling to dab and fleck and plume along your ear, and then her tap on your shoulder and a glass in your hand, and your senses reassembling to the thrill of knowing the paint never dries

After *Waterloo Bridge*, Claude Monet (1900)

The By-Product Storage Tanks

In the museum I (do we say,)—
snap?— a picture of Stella's

industrial sketch in charcoal
(the right material to make

these marks) just before
security says, no pictures,

please, sir, even with your
phone. Only later do I see

my own bare scalp reflected
in framed glass before tanks,

back-lit,—gray-scale sky ill-
uminating city-scape—

accident, kindred attempt
to contain the human.

The back of my body's
surfacing from the tank's

face. Another time I've stored
myself in some unexpected

place, in Stella's sketch,
breaking the rules,

photographing myself
trespassing into work

I've been drawn to.

After *The By-Product Storage Tanks*, Joseph Stella (1918-20)

Winter Memoir

> *"It was the only time in South Florida history that snow fell from the skies."*
> —Sun Sentinel

For years after, I thought it was a dream,
Grass and juniper bush no longer
Green but sleeved in a bell-ringing white,
Fading as its flight descended to the earthly
Pulpits of weather and school, a dark moon
City unprepared for this vision, delivered
From photographs of northern lands, or a fable
Where a girl loves her family enough
To stitch them new guises and give her skin
To the service of one lone wing.

Glazed ash, true mirage of the concrete tropics—
The first time I saw snow was in Miami, and I lifted
Both hands to measure the crook between
Who survives and who eats the bitter root.
Each leaf snapped its glass, the pond froze
To a blade reflecting the day. What I saw
Was myself, a forgotten pin, afraid and hoping
For better. What I said was *here, whole as a book.*

After *Nightfall in Snow at Terashima Village*, Kawase Hasui (1920)

The Old Bridge

The old bridge arches across
the blue-green river, where ink-
black fish swim like a string

of dark, dreamless days.
When we close our eyes,
we're carried to the other side—

a garish fantasy
of pink clouds, orange
roofs and purple paths. Sleep-

walkers, we shrug our shoulders
against the day and fill
our silver pails until

they gleam with dream water.
When night falls, we
are free

as spread-armed shirts pinned
to a moonbeam.
We dance in a delirious wind.

After *Alte Brücke*, Max Pechsein (1921)

Mother's Golden Voice

I began my assent a fugitive of night;
only the stars offered a twinkle
to my flight away from home.
When the sky turns a sorry blue,
I realize I have never been alone.

The golden voice in my head
so audible, as if mother clings
to my auburn hair, a tug of wind
she rides on my coattails.
Or am I the one who escapes
her provincial crimson legacy
a yellow light that clothes me?

I took her extra walking stick,
the cane she said would be
mine one day, passed down
from her mountain elders.

My nose points towards Sirius
determined to reach tomorrow.
In this darkness a wrinkle of white,
her sweater another parting gift.

Does she still wear the poppy skirt,
peach blouse, and are her feet

still bare because she isn't fancy
like some of her city friends.

Will she let me find my own way in the night?

After *Jeune fille en marche,* Marc Chagall (1927-28)

From Her Favorite Bench in Ménérbes, Provence, Dora Maar, Aged 87, Feeds & Talks to the Pigeons at Her Feet

I have heard it all, my sweet birds, every little crumb of gossip!
>*That old woman there: look! It's Dora Maar. Picasso's mistress!*

I hate those cruel hisses & ignorant epithets!
Do they think I can't hear them?
>*Look! There! It's Dora Maar: from the Weeping Woman painting...*

Mon Dieu—what imbeciles... I was "The Dora Maar"
long before Eluard introduced me to Picasso: Dora Maar
the activist, Dora Maar of the New Photography Movement,
Dora Maar the artist, the portraitist, the set photographer
in a Jean Renoir film!

>*The Weeping Woman, look—that's her, that's her!*

Non, non: that does not define me. If you could only
see that portrait, my doves: all angles & triangles, edges &
tortured lines — that's not me, there's no passion there,
no laughter, no *volupté!* Ah, what passion we shared
that year! It was in late '38, I remember—

only two years after that other portrait he made of me,
in '36, my favorite one, where I'm all curves & blue gazes
staring deeply at him, yet also looking away, some
have said it was in fear of seeing what would happen
to us: the wars between us, the war around us!

Ah, those wars gave us our happiest times as I
photographed him painting *Guernica* every day:

his master piece. It only took him one month,
you know, at the *rue des Grands Augustins*, in his huge
new studio. I photographed him while he painted me!

I'm the woman entering through a window, carrying
a lantern. For I brought him light & laughter, my little
pigeons, how I did! Once, just before he took me
in his arms, he let me paint a few lines on that huge
Guernica horse's neck. How we laughed that day!

Hélas, then he met that Françoise. Twenty years younger
than me. What could I do? I left. I had to. I went mad
with sorrow. So I came here, to be with God & you,
mes petits pigeons. Away from him, away from Paris...
But that portrait, with its watery background

the very color of my eyes? *That* was me! His *petite Dora*:
wide eyes & full lips, my hand about to untie my hair for him.
Pablo, that genius, my demon lover. Dead now for decades.
Ah, little birds: come closer, here, listen to me:
I was never Picasso's mistress. He was just my master. *

After *Portrait of Dora Maar (Theodora Markovich)*, Pablo Picasso (1936)
*The last line in the poem is a quote attributed to Dora Maar

Beach Riders

There was a time when I approached reality similarly
The senses took the physical and dashed it liberally, simply
With a paintbrush as whittling knife, paring revelation
Using the raw cues of objects whether plant, animal or human
To liberate life from tedious detail, from local color, and control
Free to ride a blue horse, or a greenish one on the loose beach sands
To assign the sunbathers a flesh carmine red or vermillion glow
Pain free of burn, yet heated-up like a coil on an electric stove
Then take that skin red and use it to sign your name

After *Beach Riders*, Milton Avery (1941)

Acts of Dis-conformity

Rising in sleep from sharp-edged
geometric shapes, is this song solely
herself, singing, or the song expected:
curvilinear flower, pistil and ovary?

Why not the wings of the self unwounded,
a song of being, the last and the first of many
continuously emerging? This second song
rises with the destruction of the given,

the paltry shadow against the emerging self.
Windless winds the color of sage give voice
not only to a separate being but minister
to the undiscovered, elusive self.

After *Second Song*, Kay Sage (1943)

While Looking at Chagall's Painting *Femme Cheval* at SBMA

I.
I am a horse turning into a woman
when the full moon rises
on a night where dreams become fishes
     wearing gowns and playing violins
I am a red horse roaring across the void
     converging with the Milky Way
     with my starburst gallop
     into the vast indigo sky
I burn with blood pumping from passion
     up through my hooves
     across my flanks
     into my noble head
     where I imagine the universe into existence
     the formation of galaxies
I am an explosion a billion light years away
     from stardust and moonshine
I feel the forming of my hips
     rising of my breasts   flesh singing
I hear the woman I was thundering towards
     with all my strength
In this dream theater
     swimming up from the ocean floor
     as violins play the waltz of flowers
I am a woman now dreaming she is the moon's child
     a bride to night burning with lunacy
     a mouth that speaks of truths forgotten
I am the red tongue of blue's embrace
     arms that encircle wedding

    of human and animal
    night and day
I am the in-between
    a sea maiden master musician
    an eye into your sex
    your nakedness
    your silent knowledge

II.
Touch me now
Ride me to the full moon and back
Drown a little
Let the earth pound and shake
Bare your red shimmering breasts
Your blood voice that ends all wars
Let the magic flow with your vision
Dance naked to the sound of flowers
Never cower
Howl and neigh and murmur the sacred marriage vows
Of yourself to yourself

All life is holy

III.
What you see in dreams is real
Trust in the invisibles
Honor flesh
Listen to bones
Learn every shade of blue
Don't be afraid to burn into life
Your third eye is the one that penetrates all forms
Venture to the wilderness of your body

Ride the night singing of the sea
Play every instrument you can
You are more than one thing
The deep fertile earth knows your name
Rise from the margins
You are the dreamer and the dream

IV.
I speak beyond his brush
His dream of me
I am galloping off the canvas
                into my own making

After *Horse-Woman* (Femme a Cheval), Marc Chagall (1945)

The Casting of the Spell

I draw down the moon
upon my head   her horns
slide sideways
like a tipsy smile

I draw up the earth
through my feet
my spine becomes
a bloodwood   bursts into leaf

energy courses   a horse's
mane sprouts   tail cascades
        powers meet
from my hooded head
the nelumbo blooms   awake

like birds   spirits flock
some   moon-blessed
touch my skin
hum   entranced

mighty Orishas draw near
Majalewa   Yemaya
I feel their shadows
beckon   numinous

this night the intention
is my own
its secrecy   its strength.

my finger bends
then another   now
when I pull my thumb
the spell will fly
one   two...

After *The Casting of the Spell*, Wilfredo Lam (1947)

Christine Penko

Dear Phyllis

     I feel I should have known you
living, as we did, mere blocks apart while Richard
painted his Ocean Park into panels of light & sea.
We may have ridden ponies or the carousel in Griffith Park—
me, a girl—you, already wife & muse. We both married men
named Richard & by all accounts yours was a happy marriage.

     But this isn't why I write. What troubles me
is this painting of you hanging in a museum in Santa Barbara,
the sunny town where you married. Within the prison of canvas
you sit alone & painfully erect in a room painted murkish green.
A red bleeds through its walls. Your hands, swathed to the knuckles
in the same blood red, are poised above a narrow table
as if over piano keys—yet we are not meant to hear music—
& on the checkerboard placed, not for you, but for some other,
invisible players, there are no pieces—

     & now (I must tell you the worst part)   you have no eyes.
Not a glimmer. Sockets scooped out, your husband spackled them
with blue nothing. Which causes me to to wonder why
he created this room of repentance & who he imprisoned there
before vanishing into Ocean Park's chaste light?

After *Woman and Checkerboard*, Richard Diebenkorn (1956)

Questions for the Artist

Mr. Diebenkorn
I have a few questions for you.
Is this woman you have painted
against a dark background
waiting for someone to join her
in a game of checkers?
Is it like waiting for Godot
and no one will ever come?
And why did you cover her eyes
with blue shadows
making her sightless?
She is inscrutable
blinded, alone.
She cannot see the sunset
through the window beyond.
You have reduced her
to a cipher.
Forgive my impertinence but
do you care about
this woman?

After *Woman and Checkerboard*, Richard Diebenkorn (1956)

Mono Lake

Algae saline soda lake, a million migratory birds, not far from the ghost town of my ancestors, lava fields, basin and range, a meromictic lake has layers of water that do not mix, only the ghosts see how little we are seeing, how this life and the next are stratified, unmixing, except in pockets we call picture frames, the lake is blue in my grandfather's collage, it must have been autumn, the light is sheltering, by spring the lake is marble green with photosynthesis, brine shrimp endemic, alkali flies, my grandfather's collage is redolent, a single tufa tower, a faraway island the water is swallowing, where are the shorebirds, avocets, killdeer, phalaropes, sandpipers, the collage is lineated and unequivocal, time has flattened the surface of his lake, an earthen calm, perhaps a memory, travelling with my grandmother after the war, when the devastation was a quiet undertow, would the world again erupt, or was there time now to make art, to raise a family, the aquifer seeps its dreams, calcium, carbonate, I visit the lake and ask the same questions, will there be time now, we drove down a deer path looking for craters, my husband read the map, the past is dormant, the future volcanic, I felt exaggerated on that lake shore, the wind force, the radioactive green of frothy water, inhospitable and yet, hallelujah, we belong in the unlikely, this will last, this will last, I thought the lake wind might elevate my daughter and she, like a gull, would fight the gale with her strong wings, knowing exactly where she wants to go.

After *Mono Lake #2*, William Dole (1959)

Simple Colors

This is the map of our body
that which contains us—
what seems naked deceives us
indivisible hues sheathed in rugged cloth.
We know what lies beneath.
It keeps coming back to this:
even as boys die where they fall;
their blue bodies decomposing
on concrete facades
and girls striding forth in pubescent bravado
bleed from wounds inflicted by unguarded forces
those who deign constrict their tongues.

Even as a bright mosaic of children,
shades of pink beige and brown,
suckle at the fountain of knowing
their waning innocence
draws fire from a reckless discontent
their precious hearts skipping beats
like stick figures dancing on hard ground
their open mouths choked with muted sound
their last breaths shrouded in grotesque horror.

Our mourning cries but a hollow echo.
Our inconsolable grief a muffled scream.
Where beyond the horizon might hope live?

We know women of all allegiances
who lay battered on the threshold of safe places;

their sacred vows dishonored and heaved asunder.
Yet like iridescent smoke from a sacrificial pyre
their wounded spirits still rise.
Swirling in the manner of a zephyr,
cradling grace for generations to come.

We know men who never stand to battle;
who never declare their brother a foe.
Men who worship life as treasure;
who never prize their purpled hearts.
Men who weep bold tears when others die.
Men who gently tend memorial gardens.

On some far hill, a dim golden beam is reflected
In some sequestered place, a flickering light maintains
and there, men of all stations
women of all creeds
descendants of all ancestry
life after life hold fast to an eternal vision.
The mingled colors
the vibrancy of our universe
the vein of our existence
the map of our one body
the container of us all.

After *Simplex Munditis*, Hans Hoffman (1962)

Fragments

Her cupboard a jumble,
orphaned teacups and saucers,
mismatched like her lovers,
a chip here, a crack there,
unfixable disasters
like a spilled jigsaw puzzle,
scattered, missing pieces.

Her first and favorite teacup,
cobalt blue and winter white
with lovebirds suspended in the sky,
delicately draped trees, lovers on a bridge.

Each morning she rises with ritual grace,
pads barefoot across cold kitchen tiles,
prepares steaming tea for her stubble-faced swain,
smiles doe-eyed, drinks in happiness,
like lovers forever painted on a teacup.

Vapors of steeping Sencha tease her nose,
warmth of porcelain kisses her lips.
An early sun peeks in the window,
its yellow fingers stream across oilcloth,
touch the note he left.

Raging eyes ignite red, hands quake,
the blue and white cup slips through her hand,
shatters into tiny pieces.
Arms flail, she grabs and breaks every other teacup,

slams the cupboard door,
vows a Wabi-sabi way,
wilts into the colored shards,
weeps into the Blue Willow saucer.

After *Simplex Munditis*, Hans Hoffman (1962)

Heritage

The Earth dreams me
When she dreams me in color—
I am everything blue
I am glorious with sky
brilliant with birds: Bluebird, Bluejay, fairy wren.
I fly with wings of indigo lace I dyed myself,
such is the joy available in blue.

Add iron and I am grieving
All is the color of ash and sand, of bruises.
Children died while singing today.
Iron, like death, makes its claim.
changes everything.
This is how an Earth dream transmutes.
You add the mordant.

Come to me, says Earth, be dreamed again
in pomegranate, peach with fuzzy cheeks.
Grapes designed to be wine
climb the greyed twist of apricot limbs.
The freshness of asparagus
green on buttered toast.

I am dreamed by the Earth,
birthplace and Mother.
I belong wherever she dreams me.
Her colors are my true catechism,
My eyes are her forever.

After *Simplex Munditis*, Hans Hoffman (1962)

Galaxy Apple

Plucked
        out of the vastness
                from celestial orchard
the apple gleams
        a lantern in burnished night.
Pin-pricked light-freckled
                curves shimmer
      like nebulae.

A universe so contained—
                          nestled
into my cupped hands.
                I touch
my lips to the stars.

After *The Galaxy Apple*, Paul Caponigro (1964)

Black Panther Ghazal

> *The minute we take a picture we become political.*
> —Pirkle Jones

If shooting a photograph   is surely political,
can even selfies truly   eschew the political?

Newton's trial before a   jury of eleven Whites and
one Black man, like a   scene in a movie political.

Black men on the stark   white stone steps in black leather jackets,
holding "Free Huey"   flags... A shot purely political.

The fierce panther on   the banner undulates with the breeze,
poised to down an unwary   baboon, reads political.

'County Court House'—   the words engraved in stone, the serif font,
deep cut, wide circular   O's, imbue the political.

Black berets, sunglasses,   steel/tempered glass security
doors, stern looks—the   scene portrayed, unduly political.

The art deco grill before   the dark windows diffuses
the sun through shaded   glass, so moodily political.

5,000 protesters surround the   Black Panthers
on the steps to support Newton.   Cue the political!

In April, three months before this   shot was taken, so was
the Black preacher in Memphis   for hewing political.

Kin of unarmed Black citizens,   and boys slain by armed law
enforcement officers now build   a movement political.

Alexander,   rabid anti-Levitical,
predictably,   backs the dissolutely political.

After *Black Panther Demonstration, Alameda County Court House, Oakland, California During Huey Newton's Trial*, Pirkle Jones (1968)

Found You

Accidentally
In the corner of the museum
Image familiar
Composed of those
Tiny puzzle piece fragments
Your name bold on the tag
Creator of Mr. Nobody

The somebody I know
His presence pale and tall
Empty
Lights above superimpose
My reflection
On his non-face

Feeling a tug
One visit you told us
Your stuff was junk
Cast it in the trash
Returned to square one
Began drawing coloring book style
Painted far out of the lines
Added poems   twists   puns
Tongue in cheek
And along came Mr. Nobody

While the creek creaked
And the sky turned over
You were praised as

Father of the West Coast
Funk School of Art

Now that Nobody
Dunce Cap raised high
Has got the world by the tail
Too many Somebodies
Left behind
Unless I'm Ms. Understanding

After *Mr. Nobody*, William T. Wiley (1975)

Waves

There are moments in the trough

When the thought of tenderness
A memory of your kindness

Could just as easily
Pull me into the undertow

As keep me afloat.

After *Untitled (Ocean), from the portfolio, "Untitled,"* Vija Celmins (1975)

Movement

His eyes sometimes take on this green color
hazel they call it
watching them change to gold
I fall easily under their sway
like looking into the depths of this painting
in front of me, falling again
taken in by what seems to be gentle light
either playing on water or peeking through trees
something moving, pulling me in
never down under leafs decay
but inside its resurgence
copper bright, like the pennies we'd dive for
returning to the surface again to see the world
still shimmering there, waiting
before one more descent to the source.

After *Green Sway*, Helen Frankenthaler (1975)

Bicentennial Bandwagon

What a cast of characters are on board today!

The dour Redcoat, and his cigar store companion,
that trick cyclist riding a high wire above the cracked

liberty bell, the individual in back wearing a star-

spangled dress who might be Betsy Ross—
or possibly Caligula. What a ride! What a ride!

And our driver—Jim Crow, the others call him—

is smiling all the while, though not at his lunatic passengers,
or his swaybacked horse, or even the fireworks

exploding across the summer sky. No,

what amuses him is the prospect of that distant cliff.
Don't worry, though, this bandwagon travels slowly—

the road's end looks at least forty years away.

After *Bicentennial Bandwagon (Red Grooms), from the portfolio, "Spirit of Independence, Kent Bicentennial,"* Red Grooms (1975)

More Now to Be Innocent Of

There's no borderland better
than a bed, what with bodies
slipping into each other like
waking sinking into sleep,
and I can feel my skinny body
slip like a knife into her perfume.
Then at some sudden hour
it's morning, a new day,
a hopeful we have no problem
crushing like a roach lost
in all that sudden unwanted light.

This might be better noir,
but at best it's full moonlit,
and the red bedspread
unrealistic and suggestive,
a *corrido* penned by a gringo,
then serialized and sold
on the labels of canned pintos.
It might be better neon,
but the trailer's no motel.
If only a vacancy sign
leaked its carmine glow
into the room like blood
inking its way into a bathtub.
That would be something.

Instead we've got words
in place of all that isn't.
How hard it is to see
and not say. Supposedly,

four people walked in
and only two walked out
but without any of them
it's a true murder mystery.

When I get to the border,
I hope the clues are better
than blood smudges that
might just be a sloppy hand,
an artist's refusal to deny
how much is dull process.
Better than one rock too big
to be inside a room without
some malicious purpose,
especially with the bed angled
up off the floor as if it wanted
out itself, as if it knew
the problem in hard and fast
is how quick fast manifests.

So here's how I see it: a grave
like cherry pie shoveled
out of the bed, an artful horror,
the red spread pouring
to the floor, yet a reminder
of something you might order
in a diner you only wish existed.
Or perhaps didn't. That border
we never know we cross
until we do and can't find the bodies.

After *Bed With Ditch, from the 'Juarez' Suite*, Terry Allen (1976)

Monument for K.W.

It is a circus act you pull off every day
High above our heads
Balancing on a high wire on skates
Roller Skates and that silly dunce hat
Not to mention that 12 foot beam
With the globe—
the weight of the world
On each end
Some sort of Quantum trick

I'm tired of looking up
The sky has those colors
That precede a storm
You know all washed out
Like me

Wake me when you come down
I'll be in the cot
The one directly underneath you
As if it might be a safety net

After *Monument for K. W.*, William T. Wiley (1978)

Brute

Put this face
in the breakfast nook,
or behind a wheel,
or talking to someone who is 3

This face
in the living room dining room bedroom bath room,
behind the desk he wants a word with you,
leering in the windshield and you are already dragged
by the swagger that says you're his

Put this face
on the body of someone who is 7
laden with fury and frantic
why doesn't it work,
everyone near
meaning the worst
until conclusions are only
what's standing

after years
of sitting in classrooms
barely understandable,
out to recess in danger

then back home
where every day rages
from the ones
unavoidable

until when finally grown
this face has become
the only country it knows

After *A Hollow Gesture*, Robert Arneson (1980)

Cementerio (Cemetery)

Release the birds
for there is no release
from the gravity of loss
and the weight of the sky.
A pillow word.
A floating woman:
bundle of sticks in hand,
one pointing upwards
like a staff, the
Princess of Pentacles,
unrepentant.
Translation dissolves
into whitewashed walls,
like the meaning
of time between my
language and yours.
In a world black and white
walls melt into sky.
Your body is a shadow,
the shape of a womb, or a tomb.
The unsayable remains behind
a wall, or becomes a photograph,
an image no tide could hold back.
Knowledge, a seduction,
like flocks of swallows breathing;
expanding and contracting,
back and forth
in the sea of the air.
Vacant window frames

entrances to other worlds—
a shell broken, a kernel eaten.
A widow wears her
bedclothes inside out,
sleeps with a bundle of sticks,
dreams of a wine-dark
sea of birds.

After *Cementerio (Cemetery), Juchitán, Oaxaca*, Graciela Iturbide (1988)

Listen to the Ancestors

watch the zizi soar
        over your ancestral village
                believe these wise owls
                      etch truth
in the future past

pluck the wing's white feather
        and hold it in your hand
                admit you have always
                      been jealous of flight
make it your talisman

understand the ancestor's last words
        were salvaged from the ocean floor, burdened
                by stones of waste, and whispered
above hidden graves

learn that all things begin in thought
        intention   talon   truth
                listen to the warnings of impending evil
                      for all that has transpired
will come again

wherever you migrate
        realize the zizi will find you
                like beaks chasing mice in the field

let wisdom paint your story in a single brush stroke
                recognize the language of the terrible
                              how it takes root in darkness
                                            watch fear and terror
blossom into shame and guilt

dream the deaf will hear wind created by wings
        dream the blind will see the golden eyes of the other
                dream the unfeeling will feel torn by talon and beak

awaken from your slumber
                and know we are all descendants of one mother
                              understand you have left Africa
but Africa has not left you

After *The Sleep of Reason Produces Monsters*, Yinka Shonibare (2008)

Index of Artists & Poets

Alexander, Ronald A.	58	Longo, Perie	60
Allen, Terry	65	Luschei, Glenna	21
Arneson, Robert	68	Miller, Kathee	44
Avery, Milton	42	Monet, Claude	32, 33
Bailey, Alison M.	31	Moon, Delia	14
Benjamin, Rick	34	Moran, Thomas	27
Bortman, Gudrun	57	Osborn, Enid	25
Bosselaar, Laure-Anne	40	Pagés, Christina M.	23
Braff, Steve	13	Palacio, Melinda	38
Brown, John George	22	Pechsein, Max	37
Brown, Mary	24	Penko, Christine	49
Caponigro, Paul	57	Picasso, Pablo	40
Celmins, Vija	62	Quinn, Peg	22
Chagall, Marc	38, 44	RBS	15
Chiavelli, Susan	72	Remington, Frederick	31
Chilcott, John	33	Ridland, John	19
Davis, Fran	29	Rodin, Auguste	25
Davis, Pamela	17	Rolle, Sojourner Kincaid	52
DeCanio, Carol	68	Rousseau, Henri	30
Diebenkorn, Richard	49, 50	Saccoccio, Linda	42
D-Napoleon, Natalie	70	Sage, Kay	43
Dole, William	51	Shields, Susan	50
Elliott, John	43	Shonibare, Yinka	72
Ernest, Kimbrough	62	Signac, Paul	29
Flanagan, Tessa	47	Starkey, David	64
Frankenthaler, Helen	63	Stella, Joseph	34
Freericks, Mary	32	Strohl, Roslyn	56
Grooms, Red	64	Sullivan, Kevin Patrick	67
Harnett, William Michael	19	Sullivan, Patti	63
Hasui, Kawase	36	Thomas, Daniel	37
Hoffman, Hans	52, 54, 56	Tissot, James	23
Iturbide, Graciela	70	Trelles, Emma	36
Janssen, Luci	54	Wiley, William T.	60, 67
Jones, Pirkle	58	Willis, Paul J.	27
Keith, William	21	Yatchisin, George	65
Klein, Gabriella Josephine	51	Yost, Chryss	30
Lam, Wilfredo	47		

www.ingramcontent.com/pod-product-compliance
Lightning Source LLC
Chambersburg PA
CBHW020624300426
44113CB00007B/773